M000120704

Famous & Fun Pop Duets

6 Duets for One Piano, Four Hands

Carol Matz

Famous & Fun Pop Duets, Book 5, contains carefully selected popular hits from movies, radio and television. The duets are arranged in equal parts for intermediate pianists, and are written for one piano, four hands. The melody often shifts between *primo* and *secondo,* creating interesting parts for both players. Enjoy your experience with these popular hits!

Carol Matz

Alfred Music Publishing Co., Inc.
P.O. Box 10003
Van Nuys, CA 91410-0003
alfred.com

ISBN-10: 0-7390-4960-7
ISBN-13: 978-0-7390-4960-0

If I Only Had a Brain

(Featured in the M-G-M Picture "The Wizard of Oz")

Secondo

Music by Harold Arlen
Lyric by E.Y. Harburg
Arranged by Carol Matz

If I Only Had a Brain

(Featured in the M-G-M Picture "The Wizard of Oz")

Primo

Music by Harold Arlen
Lyric by E.Y. Harburg
Arranged by Carol Matz

Secondo

think of things I nev - er thunk be - fore,

8va

Primo

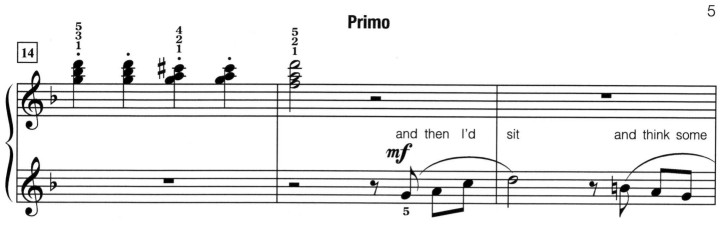

and then I'd sit and think some

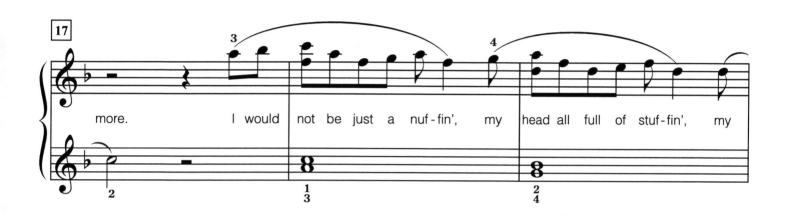

more. I would not be just a nuf-fin', my head all full of stuf-fin', my

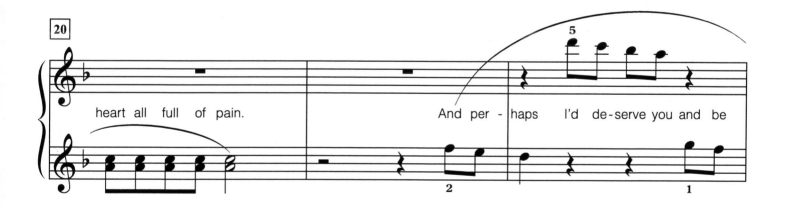

heart all full of pain. And per - haps I'd de-serve you and be

e - ven wor-thy erv you, if I on - ly had a brain.

The James Bond Theme

Secondo

By Monty Norman
Arranged by Carol Matz

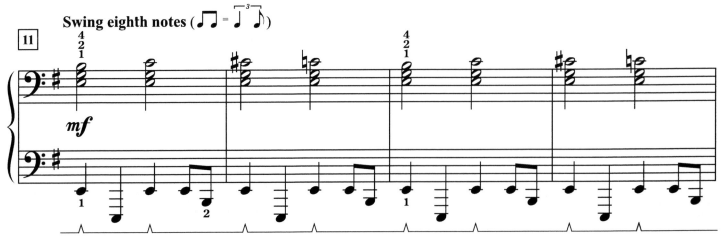

The James Bond Theme

Primo

By Monty Norman
Arranged by Carol Matz

Secondo

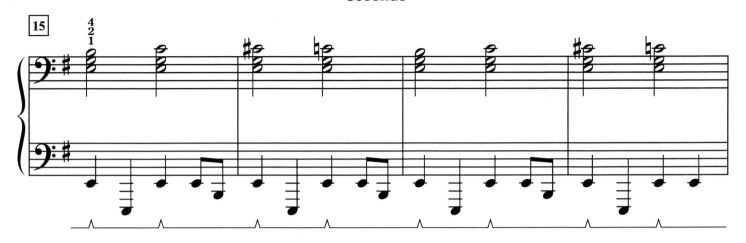

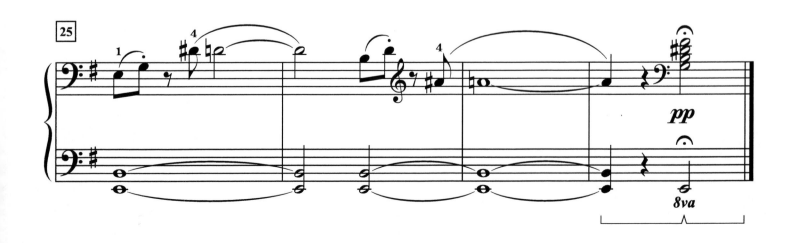

Primo

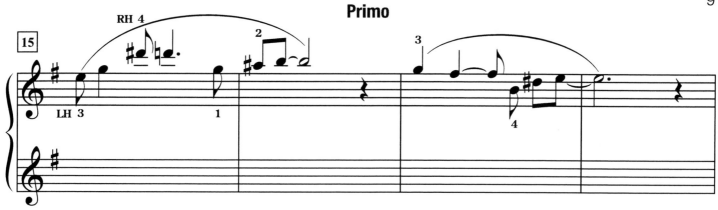

No swing

Theme from "Superman"

Secondo

By **JOHN WILLIAMS**
Arranged by Carol Matz

Medium march tempo

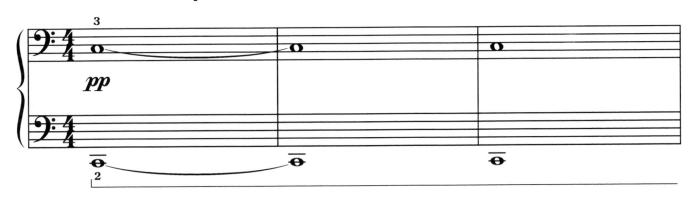

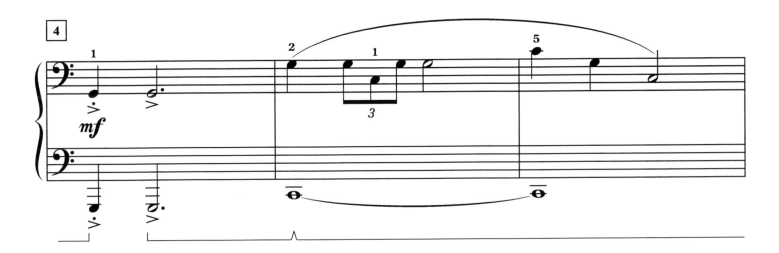

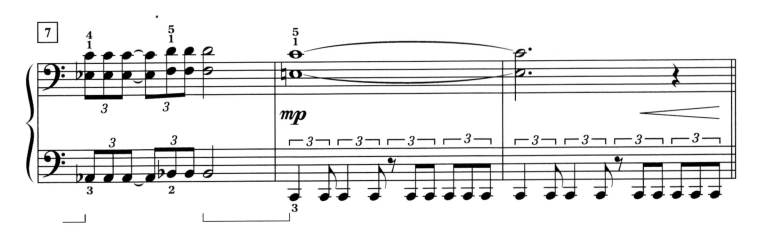

Theme from "Superman"

Primo

By **JOHN WILLIAMS**
Arranged by Carol Matz

Medium march tempo

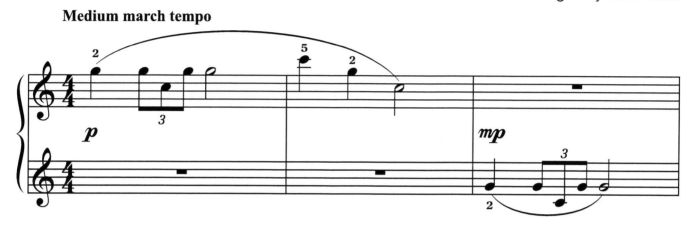

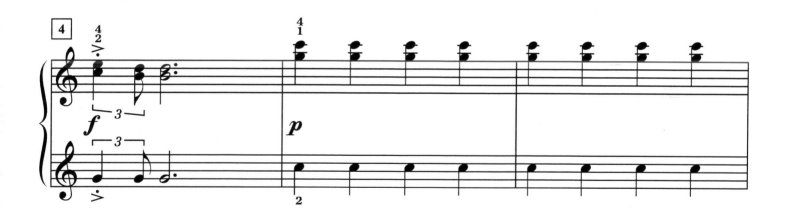

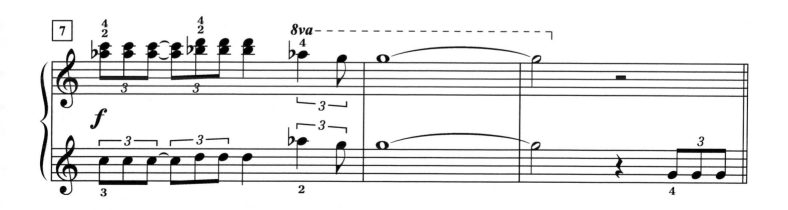

Secondo

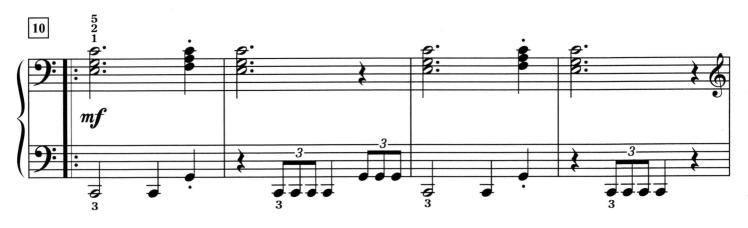

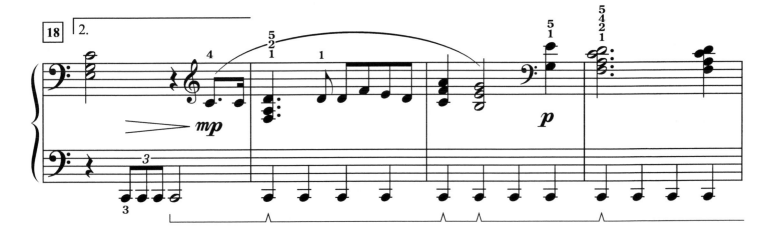

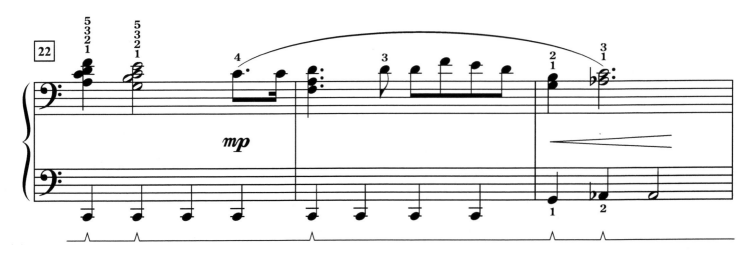

Primo

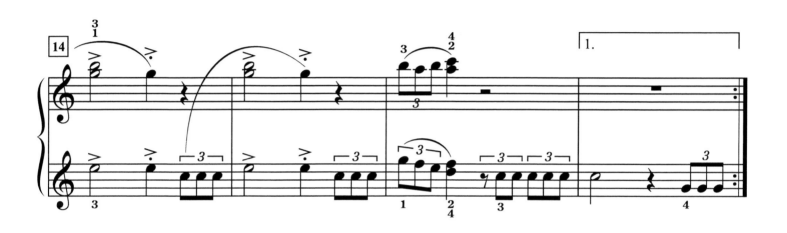

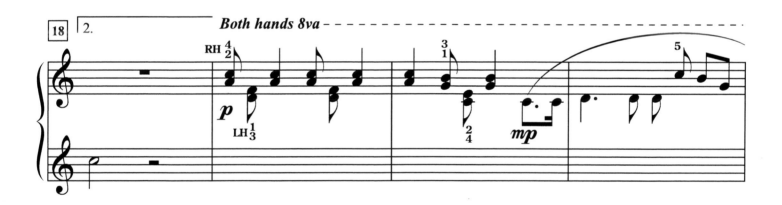

Secondo

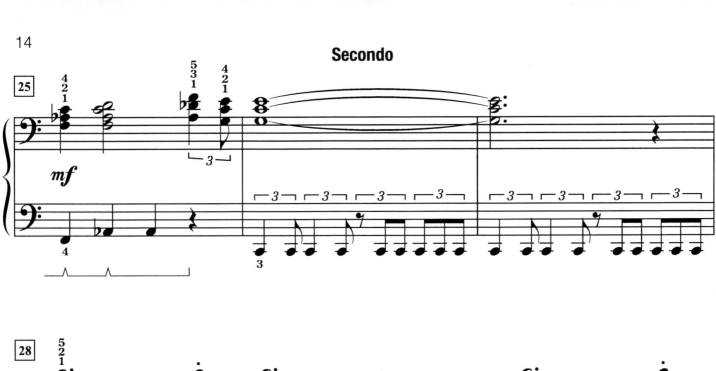

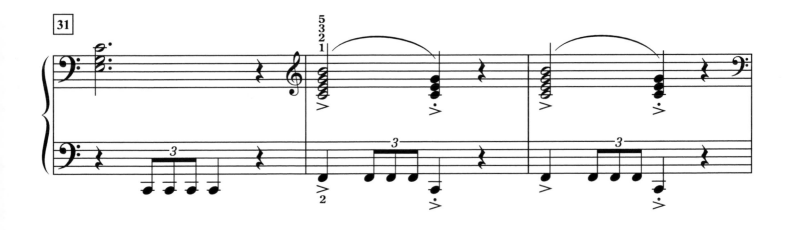

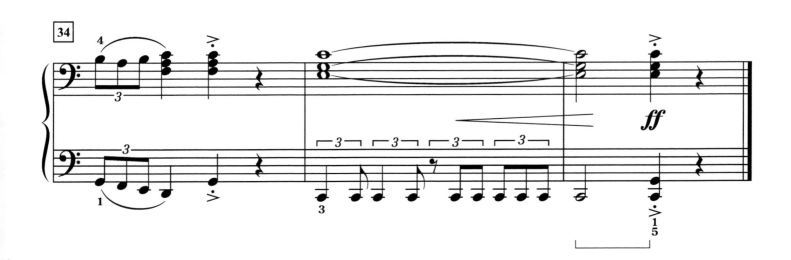

Primo

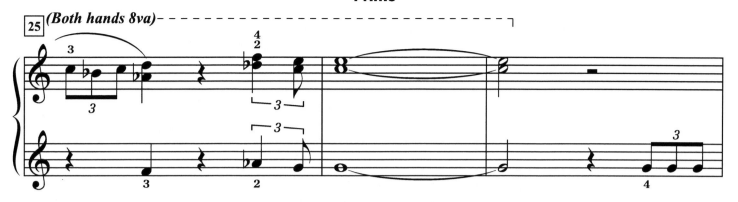

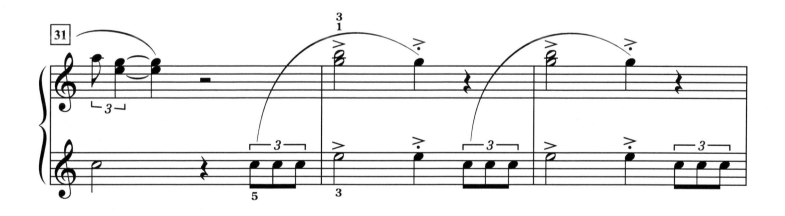

You're the One That I Want

Secondo

Words and Music by John Farrar
Arranged by Carol Matz

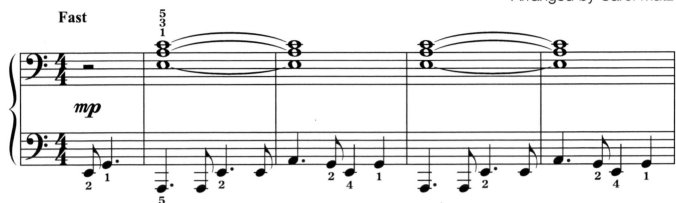

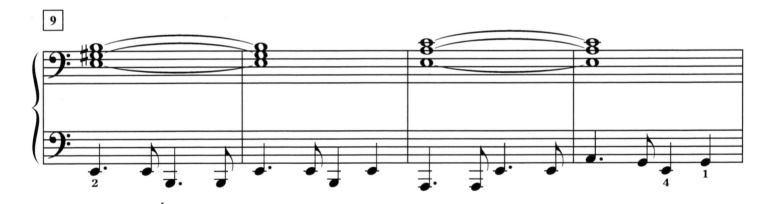

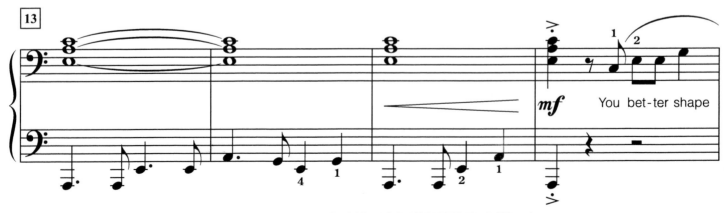

You're the One That I Want

Primo

Words and Music by John Farrar
Arranged by Carol Matz

Secondo

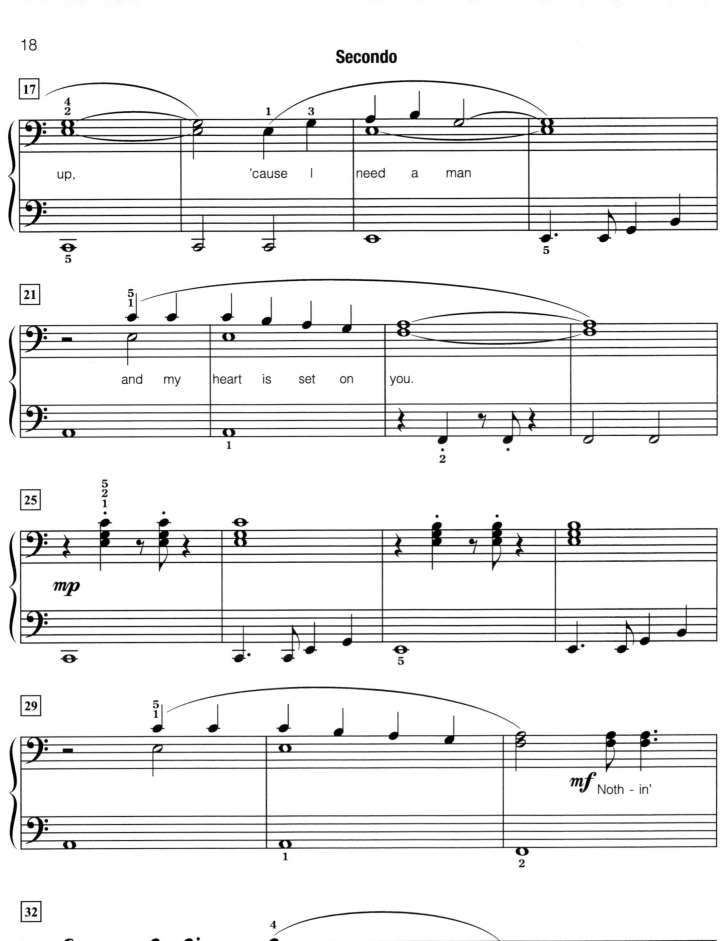

up,   'cause I   need a   man

and   my   heart is   set on   you.

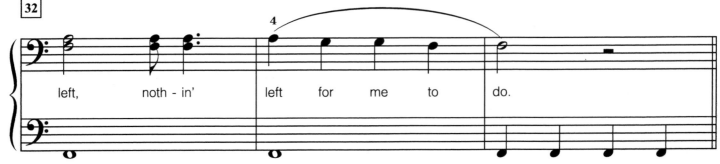

left,   noth - in'   left   for   me   to   do.

Secondo

Star Wars®
(Main Title)

(from the Twentieth Century Fox Motion Picture "Star Wars®")

Secondo

By **JOHN WILLIAMS**
Arranged by Carol Matz

Star Wars®
(Main Title)

(from the Twentieth Century Fox Motion Picture "Star Wars®")

Primo

By **JOHN WILLIAMS**
Arranged by Carol Matz

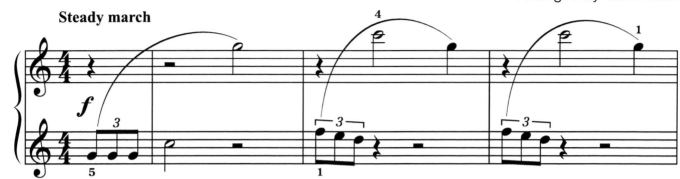

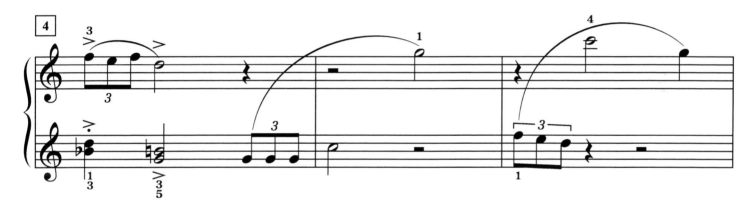

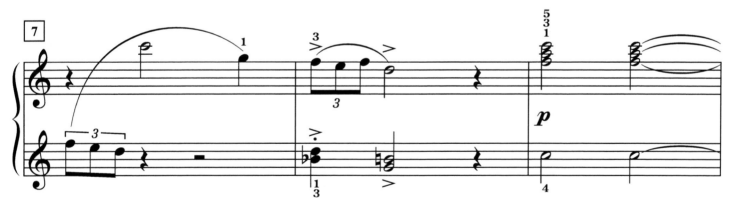

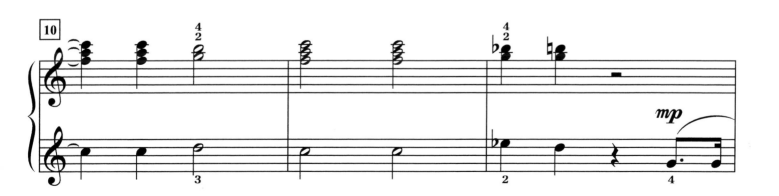

Secondo

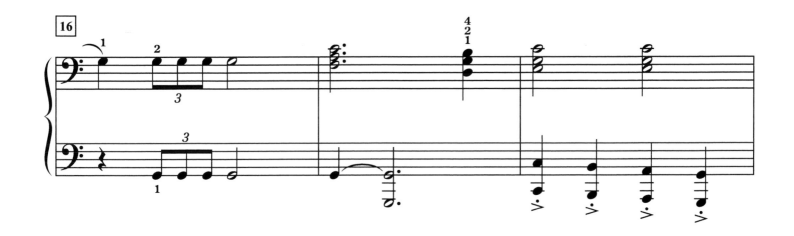

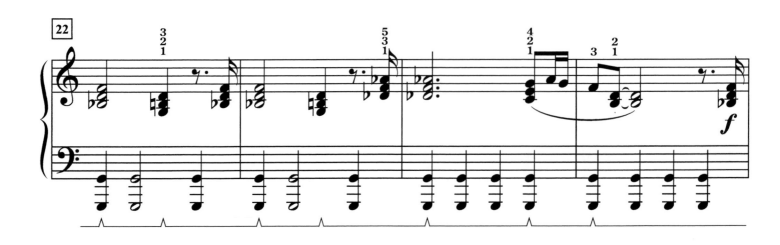

Primo

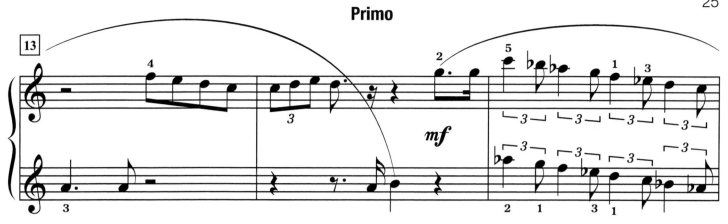

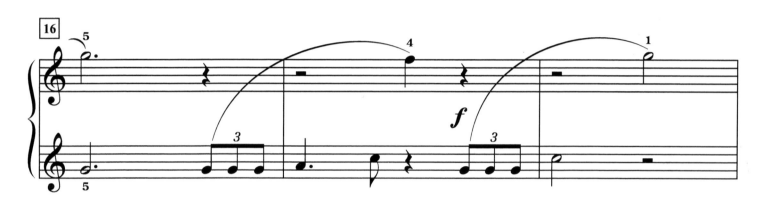

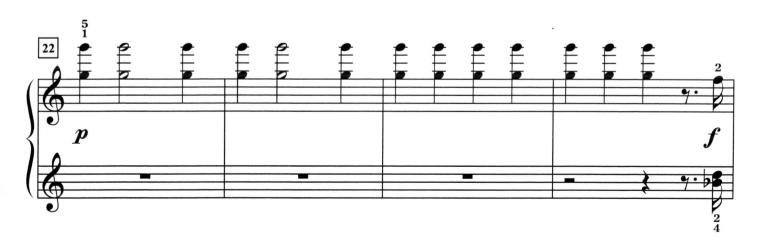

Secondo

Primo

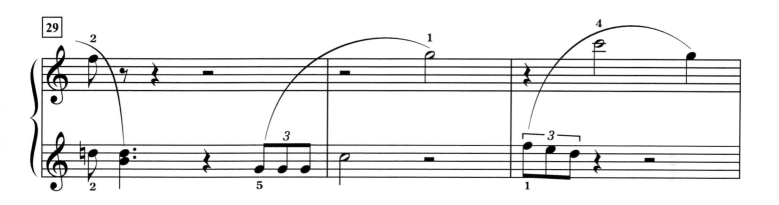

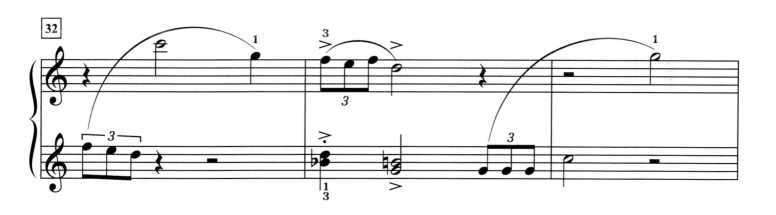

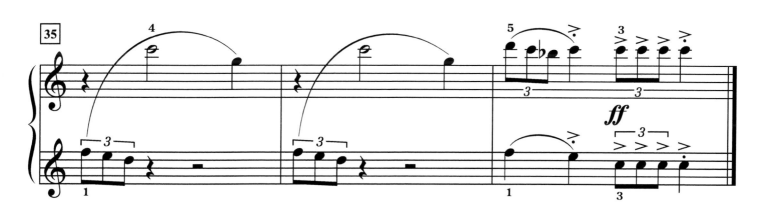

Cruella De Vil

(from Walt Disney's "101 Dalmatians")

Secondo

Words and Music by Mel Leven
Arranged by Carol Matz

Cruella De Vil

(from Walt Disney's "101 Dalmatians")

Primo

Words and Music by Mel Leven
Arranged by Carol Matz

Secondo

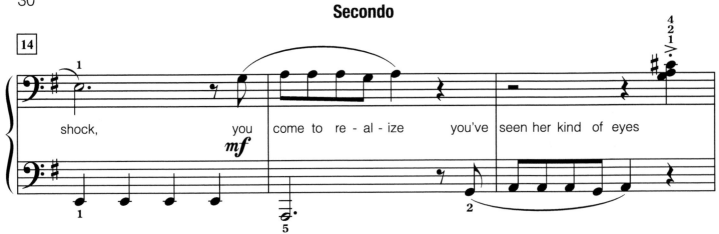

shock, you | come to re-al-ize you've | seen her kind of eyes

mf

watch-ing you from un-der-neath a rock!

f

mp

8va----------------------

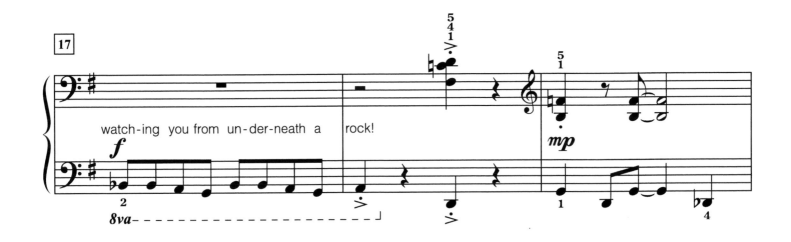

mf

f

Primo

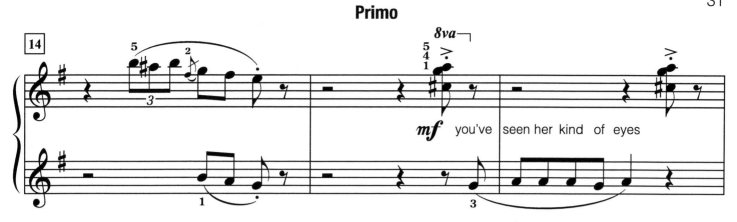

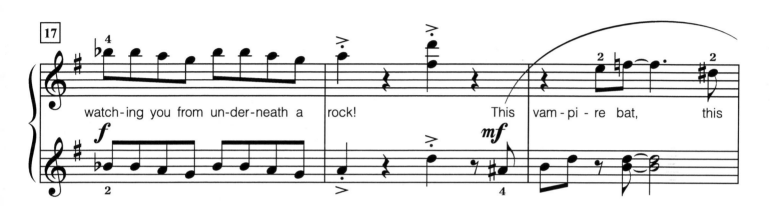

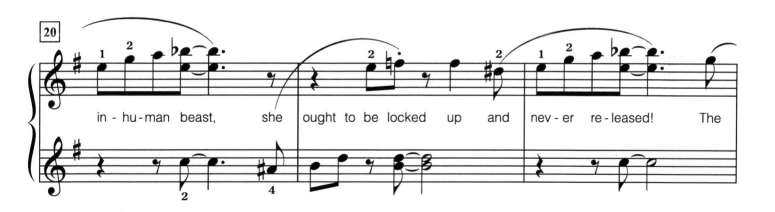

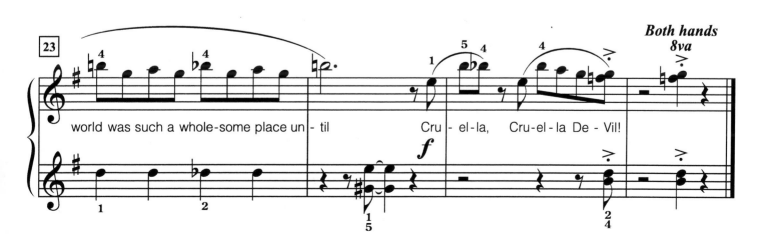